SUPER
7
PRINCIPLES
— TO —

GROW, WIN WITH PEOPLE,
BE MORE CREATIVE AND PRODUCTIVE

FRED OPIE

opie
PRESS

Published by Opie Press
Natick, MA 01760
www.FredOpie.com

First published 2020

Manufactured in the United States

ISBN 978-0-9991893-1-3

Library of Congress Control Number: 2020904745

This publication is designed to provide essential and researched information with regard to the subject discussed. It is published with the understanding that the publisher is not engaged in rendering financial, accounting, or other professional advice. If financial advice or other expert assistance is required, professional services are advised.

Cover Design: DesignStudio

Interior Design: Allan Ytac

CONTENTS

PREFACE

This book evolved out of teaching the Super Seven Principles to my students as a professor at Babson College. I taught the principles over the course of several semesters for approximately three years. After sharing a principle, I invited students to share their comments and questions. Each time I taught the Super Seven, I made changes and improvements based on the feedback I received. Over the years, my students have shared that learning the Super Seven has been a tremendous help to them.

If you have success in something, do you know why, or is it an accident? If you do something and you make a lot of money, do you know why you made a lot of money? Can you repeat it? If you had a good game in whatever sport you play, if you're a singer and you had a solo and it was excellent, do you know why? Well, I had to start thinking about that in my life. If I have had some success, to what do I attribute that success? I concluded that my successes came down to what I call my "Super Seven."

The Super Seven Principles have definitely been the formula for success that I developed to thrive on and off the field. If you apply these principles, you'll see that they're universal, and you can use them in all areas of your life.

CHAPTER 1

Evaluation and Failure

Getting the Feedback You Need to Succeed

Some folks handle feedback better than others. I first started thinking about this principle when I was a student athlete in college and I was not getting the playing time I wanted. Maybe if I had been in theater, you'd say I wasn't getting the roles I wanted. If it was business, you'd say I wasn't getting the compensation I wanted. In short, things were not going well, and I was not happy about it at all.

It took a while, but I got up the courage to go and talk to my position coach. Depending on your situation, think "commanding officer," "boss," "supervisor," "director," and so on. I said, "What do I need to do to get more playing time?" He looked at me puzzled, like, "Why don't you already know?" That's the assumption those in authority or those we report to often have: that people know what they're supposed to do. But we don't always know, even when we've been told. Sometimes what someone says and what we hear are not the same.

So I asked him, "What do I need to do?" He stuck out his hand, and he said, "I need you to work on A, B, and C." And I was like, "Wow, that's it?" I had been fixated on doing all these things that I thought he wanted, and it wasn't what he wanted at all. And that's why things weren't going well.

Evaluation is getting the feedback that you need to succeed. I got the feedback and made the changes, and then I started getting more playing time, and things began turning around for the better. We all need feedback about what we're doing wrong in order to get better. Moreover, failure is a kind of feedback. Avoiding failure, just like avoiding evaluation, means we'll never learn what we need to learn in order to be most successful.

Figure 1 That's me on the right playing defense on an unknown University of Massachusetts player at an away game at UMass in 1985

In *Mindset: The New Psychology of Success,* Carol Dweck says success is about learning, and people need honest and constructive feedback in order to learn well. She defines "constructive criticism" as feedback that helps a person understand how to improve. It's about helping a person fix something, improve something, or do a better job. We should all be seeking feedback on how to learn from our experiences and improve.[1] In his book *Failing Forward,* John C. Maxwell says, "No matter what kind of failure you experience, there's always a potential jewel of success contained in it."[2] The person in pursuit of success must to learn to view failure as a normal part of the process of achieving a goal. It's true: the more you risk failure and actually fail, the greater your chances of success. At the same time, if you're a parent, coach, or team leader, remember to use a person's accomplishments rather than their failures to weigh their potential. Help them move from sporadic brilliance toward consistent goal achieving.[3]

Evaluation Freaks Some People Out

Often, people get freaked out by evaluation situations such as, quizzes, tests, driving permit test, driving road test, SAT and ACT, tryouts, auditions, and or job interviews.

Figure 2 Frightened Soldiers, 1797, Courtesy of the Library of Congress

There is also state board of examinations to teach, practice cosmetology, plumbing, carpentry, accounting, medicine, and the law, for example. We all need to know that a person is qualified to provide a service or operate something like a car. I do not care who you are, you need feedback. You need to make sure you are on the same page with other people. When you get on the same page, things go a whole lot better.

Unless you seek feedback, you cannot improve. You can think you are doing the right thing until you get the feedback that tells you differently. In addition, you need to have a thick skin and learn not to take feedback personally. As a college professor, I give students feedback because I want them to get better.

> *"Failure is not falling down, but refusing to get up"*
> **—Navy Seal**

One of the principal reasons I've had the success I've had is because I had a lot of failure very early on in my life. I applied to five different colleges my senior year in high school. I was rejected from all five. My SATs were an absolute terrible failure, with a combined score of roughly 630. This was at a time when, just for putting your name on the paper, you got, like, two hundred points. So I had a low score. I didn't do well at all.

From this, I learned that to get ahead and to achieve my goals, I would have to seek out the information, the wisdom, and the answers necessary to move beyond failure. The experience made me like a sponge when it came to learning new information and learning how to grow.

I had a high of level of motivation. It was not a good motivation, but it was motivation nonetheless: as a high school student, I wanted to play sports in college. Now I tell people clearly that this is not how you want to be motivated to go to college. But my motivation to play college sports got me past a lot of the obstacles I faced.

Successful People Are People Who Have Failed a Lot

Successful people are people who have failed a whole lot. You have to become comfortable with failing. If you stay in a position of only doing things that you do well, you are not going to have a lot of success in life, and you are not going to have a lot of happiness either.

I'm reading a great book that I'd recommend to everyone. It's called

Failing Forward, by John C. Maxwell. It's not just a good book—it is an awesome book. And it's had a big impact on me and how I think about success and failure.

Should you play it safe? No. You have to take some risks, and you have to accept that you are going to have some failure. Failure is just a part of success. In fact, part of the recipe for success is failure. The company that created the all-purpose lubricant WD-40 named it for their fortieth failed attempt at creating a degreasing and rust protection product.

Bubble wrap came out of a 1960 failed effort to make housing insulation. It caught on as a shipping product when IBM used it to package and ship a recently developed computer. Its use in shipping made it a success.

An employee mistakenly dripped bran porridge on a stove top. The porridge cooked and cracked into flakes that tasted better than the soupy porridge. It took thirty-six iterations to perfect what became a profitable box of Wheaties, the Breakfast of Champions.[4]

Life is full of all kinds of failures, but they are only failures if you let them bring you to a halt—if you don't get up and try again. There is so much to learn from failures.

Should You Play It Safe?

Until 1977, Ty Cobb held the career record for most stolen bases. He still holds the record for unsuccessfully trying to steal a base. Experts estimate that Cobb failed over four hundred times.

Figure 3 Ty Cobb attempting to steal a base in 1912, Courtesy of the Library of Congress

Figure 4 a political cartoon depicting President William Taft failing miserably in 1911, Library of Congress

You Can Learn a Lot in the Process of Making Mistakes

I have published several books. But the first book was rejected by publishers at least fifteen times—fifteen! And what's interesting is, after those fifteen rejections, I've learned how to publish and how to get a book accepted. After that first book, I haven't had nearly as many book rejections. In fact, I don't remember the last time I submitted a book to a publisher and had it rejected. You can learn a lot in the process of making mistakes.

My book *Start with Your Gift* is a sports memoir with career advice in which I share my failures. I write about them so people can learn from my failure. I am a big believer in taking chances—calculated chances—and not being scared to fail. I think the fear of failure paralyzes a lot of people.

Recommended Evaluations

- » Psychological testing as needed

- » Yearly physical exam, including a blood test

- » Biannual dental exam

- » Yearly evaluation and reading of your will

- » Yearly car tune-up

- » Yearly fireplace inspection and cleaning

- » Yearly evaluation of progress on your short- and long-term financial goals

- » Yearly evaluation of your insurance policies: life, home and/or rental, and auto

CHAPTER 2

Communication

One of the things I know from teaching and coaching over many decades is that everyone is different. How I give feedback to one person is different from how I give it to another: that is critically important if I want to offer the people I'm giving feedback to the best possible chance of hearing what I have to say and learning from it.

The same thing is true of students or colleagues working together in groups. When you are working in a group, you have to understand each other, and you have to understand what is the best way to get your point across to each person in the group. Learning how to do this comes with experience. But for your own sake, you want to let people know the best you can how *you* learn and the best way to give *you* feedback.

There are a lot of different aspects to communication. We know that communication one-on-one, or among three people, is going to be different from when you're speaking to a group. We know that there's verbal communication, and then there's nonverbal communication. And we know that there are preferences—when is the best time, or the best way, to reach out to someone, particularly if they are really busy and have a lot on their plate. These are the kinds of things it's important to consider when you're thinking about communication.

That's one of the things I've had to think about over a long period of time, and it's something I continue to work on and learn more about. These are skills related to communication—a Super Seven Principle that asks us to think about not just *what* we're communicating but also *when, how, how much,* and *in what way* we're sharing our ideas with one another. This chapter is about the meta-aspects of communication, such as body language, timing, and ratios, more than it is about the content you share.

What Good Communication Looks Like

Carol Dweck says good communication calls for discussing conflicts without assuming someone's intentions. Good communication takes work, because it is challenging to say things accurately and to clarify your expectations. Good communication calls for providing your audience with helpful solutions instead of angry descriptions of problems alone. Good communicators keep the channels of communication open up and down the lines of an organization or team.[5]

When it comes to marriage, good communication means spouses share their thoughts instead of expecting the other to read minds. Spouses share when they get triggered and communicate their need for a time out before they say something they will regret. Good communicators are also introspective and ask themselves, *What triggered me to get so angry with my spouse?*[6]

Communication and Teams

Communication is the foundation of developing a great relationship. Author Jon Gordon says, "Communication builds trust. Trust generates commitment. Commitment fosters teamwork, and teamwork delivers results."[7] Communication prevents the spread of negative energy that can derail a team's positive growth and development. Gordon says to make communication and getting on the same page a priority. Breaking bread together or sharing a meal creates a great opportunity to communicate with members of your team, family, and or mastermind. By the way, a mastermind, which everyone should have formally or informally, is a group of people with various expertise you can consult when you need them. Schedule regular times to meet and speak with important people in your life. Meet one-on-one and or in groups and leverage technology to keep the communication lines open with members of your team. When team members and or leader become overscheduled, they start to get stressed out in the communication between them.[8]

Learning to Listen

I love expressions and quotations. So here's one of the quotations I like. I don't even remember where this one came from, but it's one of my favorites: "Empty barrels make the most noise." If you stop and think about what this means for how people communicate with each other, the metaphor is pretty interesting. It's suggesting that the people who speak the most often might have the least to say.

This idea points to another one I like: the two-to-one ratio. We have two ears and one mouth. I once heard a wise person say, "You should do twice as much listening as you do speaking." If you're doing all the talking in a conversation, you're not learning a whole lot. In meetings and in classrooms, we've all had the experience of listening as someone dominated the conversation. I often wonder, is it a sign of insecurity that this person can't be quiet and listen to other folks? Is this an empty barrel situation?

It's something to think about in your own life: Are you listening more than you're talking? Are you talking too much because you're nervous, or taking up too much space in a conversation when you could be listening and learning? Jon Gordon says great communicators put a premium on listening and analyzing what they are hearing to make the best collective decision possible. I like the way Gordon puts it: "They listen to learn and they learn to grow." Communication creates connection, connections build commitment, and committed people are more creative and productive.[9]

The following are communication-building strategies that Gordon says can help you connect with others. (I tried them, and they work.) Go around the room and ask everyone to answer the question, *If you really knew me,* _____. Ask everyone to share a defining moment from their lives.[10] I started doing ten-minute interviews with every student enrolled in my courses. Here are some of the questions I have asked over the years:

» What's the oldest history you know about your family?

» How have your eating, drinking, and exercise habits changed since you were eighteen?

» How do you keep yourself spiritually strong?

» When is the last time you cried and why?

» If you could have dinner with three people, dead or alive, who would they be and why?

» If I gave you ten million dollars to give away, what causes, organizations, and foundations would receive funding?

» What is the kindest thing someone has done for you?

» If you could have a superpower, which one would you want and why?

» What are some books on your suggested reading list?

» What advice would you give the fifteen-year-old you?

» I want you to write a book of success. Give me three chapter titles in your book.

I frame the opening of each interview with the statement, "You have the right to refuse to answer any question if you don't feel comfortable with it." That empowers the student in the process of building greater communication using the interviews. My students have shared that they enjoy this semester-long part of the class ritual.

Body Language

Another place to look at communication is body language. What is your body language communicating?

One of the things I've learned from my wife is that when I'm talking with her, I shouldn't fold my hands. It's a common pose for me, maybe modeled after people I've known in the past, but it sends the wrong body language signal to her. When I come in and cross my arms, it's almost as if I'm saying to her, "I'm upset about something."

Also, I often don't even realize what's on my forehead. So my forehead will sometimes be giving off the message that I'm angry when I'm not necessarily angry. I always have to tell folks, particularly my wife, "If you think I'm angry, ask me. Because most of the time I'm not." Sometimes I'm just thinking about something and don't realize what my face is actually saying to the other person. But this is a reminder that body language is really important, and it's something we can learn to pay attention to in order to be better communicators.

Culture is important, too: we have to be sensitive to the different cultures of the people we're talking to, particularly around food. What you do in one culture when you like something or don't like it might be different from what you do in another culture. In some cultures, if you fold your legs and show the sole of your foot to the people you're eating with, it's offensive. In some cultures, turning your back on somebody or refusing to shake hands is a terrible thing to do. So we need to remember that body language is a way of communicating, and to watch our body language, but we also need to keep in mind that what we do with our bodies means different things to different people, and we have to be sensitive to that. Ask yourself, "What am I communicating with my body? Is it what I want to be communicating?" We need to keep ourselves open to feedback and failure in this area, and to be willing to change when someone tells us that our body language is not matching up with what we want to be communicating.

We can also make deliberate decisions about our body language as a way of communicating. There is a technique I use that you might want to keep in your toolbox for the future. It's great to want to work around colleagues, but sometimes you have colleagues who will constantly try to communicate when you're trying to get work done. When I work with my door closed, the message is, "I'm busy." And that works a lot of the time. But when people come to me and I'm really busy, and maybe the closed door wasn't enough for them to get the message, I will meet them at the door and stand in the doorway. My message is, "I can't talk. I'm busy right now. Let's schedule a time for you to come back and talk when I know I can give you my undivided attention." This is an example of using body language to communicate a boundary. It's not that you don't care about people, but you want to make sure it's clear that this isn't a good time to talk.

The Sandwich

Just as important as your body language is the ratio of positive to negative feedback you share with others. I've already introduced the two-to-one ratio, which tells us to listen twice as much as we speak. But here's another ratio related to communication to consider: for every negative, you have to communicate at least one positive. Think of it as a sandwich: you start out with something positive, you give the feedback or the evaluation, which could be a little negative, and then you conclude with another positive. So it's just like a sandwich with the bread on the top, the filler, and then the bread at the bottom. Positive, rough, and then positive. The sandwich is a way of communicating that makes evaluation or feedback easier for the person you're talking with to accept.

Figure 5 Sandwiches for shift workmen at Consolidated Aircrafts, 1941, Courtesy of The Library of Congress

What's Your Preferred Method of Communication?

As someone with severe ADHD who knows other people who also have it, I can tell you this: we can't stand getting texts. For whatever reason, texting is labor-intensive and becomes extremely frustrating for me. I have to remind people all the time, and there are some people who will send texts that look like letters to Dear Abby. I have to tell those people to find another way to communicate with me. I have to do this in a diplomatic way, of course. But if you've got something long you want to communicate—with me, at least—put it in an email.

This is just to say, it's a good idea to let people know your preferred method of communicating. Is it email? Is it Snapchat? Is it Facebook? Whatever it is, just let people know what works best for you and find out what works best for them. Communication is a two-way street.

Time

Connected to this point is another question: What is the best time to reach you? I'm a pretty early riser. I don't want to be disturbed first thing in the morning, because there are some vital tasks I'm trying to get done. If someone were to come and try to have a conversation with me during that early time of the morning, I'm not going to want to talk to them. I'm not going to answer emails or look at emails during that time. And more than likely if someone calls my phone, I'm just going to let it go to voicemail.

Let people know not only the best *way* to reach you, but also the best *time* to reach you. Some folks are night owls, so they do their best work in the evening. There's nothing wrong with that—unless you're working with a team and you don't let your team members know. For example, you tell the people you're working with, "I have a class during X, Y, Z time," or "I'm at work during X, Y, Z time," and they email something to you or text something to you and don't hear anything but crickets, they might get a little irritated. But if you say, "Hey, the best time to reach me is during this window," you'll get a much more positive response.

I have a strategy for timing communication that you might want to consider using yourself. I have a lot of friends scattered all over the country. Before I get into the car for a long drive, for example, I'll send out a message to some of my friends and say, "Hey, I'm traveling today during this three-hour window. If you have an opportunity, I'd love to catch up with you." And then I get a bunch of phone calls during that ride, which makes the ride a whole lot easier and a whole lot more enjoyable—plus, I have a chance to catch up with my friends.

To take the opposite example, one of my friends just the other day said, "Hey, I haven't heard from you in a long time." He's constantly sending me this type of message. I don't know what his job situation is, but it was a pretty intense part of my work schedule when I just didn't have a lot of extra time. What I said was, "I'll get back to you." So I have some travel coming up, and I will reach out to him and say, "Hey, look, are you available during X, Y, and Z time?"

Telling people your preferred time to communicate is really important, because it sets you and them up for more positive and successful interactions.

Public Speaking and Writing

As a person who has a podcast, I interview a lot of people. One of the common questions I ask my guests is, "Now that you've been out of school for a decade, two decades, three decades, four decades sometimes, what do you think was the most important course?

Figure 6 Elizabeth Gurley Flynn giving a speech at the, I.W.W. Strike Headquarters, Paterson, New Jersey, 1913, Courtesy of the New York Public Library

Figure 7 Booker T. Washington speaking in Atlanta, Georgia in 1916, Courtesy of the New York Public Library

What should be a required course to graduate from college to get ready for the real world?" These are people who are movers and shakers now in their careers—very successful people who hire all the time, who do deals all the time, venture capitalists, all kinds of folks—and the most common thing they respond with is, "Communication. Public Speaking. Writing."

A lot of people, whether they be students or well-known adults being interviewed in the media, cannot speak to save their lives. There is an overreliance on fillers: uh, like, um, ah. What happened? Did they not take a public speaking course? Are they terrified of speaking? There's nothing worse than hearing a poor speaker.

I make a living as a public speaker, whether it be teaching in a classroom or giving lectures, and I can offer this advice for how to move beyond using fillers. First, try pacing yourself. If you tend to speak quickly, be intentional and decide not to do that. Try pausing in your head, making sure you know what you want to say next. These strategies will help slow you down and make your speech more deliberate, which gives you a chance to know what you want to say before you say it. The result will be that the people listening to you have a more positive experience. They'll hear what you're trying to say more clearly, and they'll be much more likely to absorb the information and respond well.

Conclusion

Communication can be complicated, because so much depends on the context: Who are you communicating with? What are trying to say, and what are saying nonverbally? When is it the best time for you to have a difficult conversation, and when is it the best time for the other person to hear what you need to say? But the important principle to remember is that you have the ability to ask questions, learn, and adapt in order to become a better communicator. Like anything complex, good communication requires study, practice, making mistakes, getting feedback, and more practice. Be introspective about your communication preferences and style, and think about ways you can grow and become a more caring and effective communicator.

» When you have the opportunity to keep your mouth closed and listen, take advantage of it.

» Share a compliment and encouragement with others as often as possible.

» Congratulate people for little and big accomplishments daily.

» A regular of time of prayer helps you communicate better with others.

» When you have the option, avoid talking with those who talk over you.

» Read positive affirmations out loud to each morning and evening to yourself. (For example, *I am caring and courageous, happy and healthy, organized and on time.*)

» For the next twenty-four hours, find something positive to say about everyone.

CHAPTER 3

Planning

Success requires clear and precise planning. Your plan needs to include details such as when, where, and how. In addition, you need to include a follow-through and follow-up contingency.[11]

Here's another tip: the probability of successful planning increases when you commit to practicing visualization. Visualization is something people have done for years and something I did as an athlete. I played defense in the sport of lacrosse. When my coaches assigned me to cover a particular player, I studied an opponent's tendencies. Then I made time to get alone and quiet and created a mental simulator in which I would play defense in all kinds of different game scenarios, running them over and over again in my head. Doing this made the actual live game against that player much easier.

Remember, make your plan, commit to it, have a strategy to follow through and follow up on the plan, and make time to visualize executing the plan in your mental simulator until you can carry it out in your sleep. All of this is important. But it means nothing if you don't know what you should plan to do daily, weekly, monthly, and so forth. In the next section, I will give you a method to prioritize your work. Each morning, you need to make a list of what you want to do each day. Creating a list of ABCs and MITs is a strategy that has helped me to organize and thereby simplify my life.

The ABCs

If you were to get an inside look at my life, you would see that I have priorities just like everybody has priorities, but my priorities are actually written down. I learned this from a book I read many years ago by a guy named Stephen Covey. His book is called *Seven Habits of Highly Effective People*. I handed the teenage version to my children about the time they entered high school. It's called *Seven Habits of Highly Effective Teenagers*.

Covey explains that highly effective people understand their priorities. They understand what's vital. If something is vital, that means that I am going to give it an A in my daily task list. If it's important, it's going to get a B. If it's nice, it'll get a C. All the things I do today, or any day, have priorities, so they may be an A. They may be an A1, A2, A3, but they're prioritized. It really makes my life very simple when I have to decide what I'm going to do, because we all have twenty-four hours a day. What are we going to do with that time?

Do You Have Your Priorities in Order?

One of the most important things to prioritize, which people tend to not give the priority it deserves, is sleep. You have to know how much sleep your body needs. Many accidents and problems in life happen because of sleep deprivation. When you look at studies of airplane or automobile crashes, you find there's a close correlation between someone being sleep-deprived and having an accident. Sleep is a high priority. I try to make sure that, at a minimum, I get six and a half hours of sleep every night. There are times when I can't do that, but to the best of my ability, that's a priority.

Another priority for me is taking care of myself spiritually. I make sure that I have a vibrant and strong spiritual life, because when the stuff hits the fan, not having a spiritual backstop can be problematic.

There are other things that are vital to me. My relationship with my wife is an example. In fact, my wife has priority over my kids. My kids have priority over my brother and my immediate family at this point in my life. The only living member of my immediate family who's still alive is my older brother, who is sixteen months older than me. But when I rank my relationship priorities, I begin with my spiritual relationship and my relationship with my wife, followed by my relationship with my kids, then my brother. It doesn't mean he's not important. I'm just talking about priorities. And if you keep those priorities in mind, it really makes life easier.

The next thing down for me in priorities is taking care of my body. I prioritize a strong spirit, a strong body, and a strong mind. These are all vital for me. And you'll notice that I haven't even gotten to what I do for a career. I'm just dealing with A-level priorities, because I've realized that if I take care of those A-level parts of my life, the other parts will flourish. One way of figuring out if something is an A-level priority is to ask what happens if you fail to take care of it. If you don't tend to the high-priority parts of your life, the other parts of your life will begin to go downhill.

B-level priorities include my relationships with people who are important to me. Those are Bs. C-level priorities—the "nice" things I want to accomplish on any given day—are actually the things I need to do for my occupation. It's not that it's not important, but when you look at *priorities*, it's only nice. It's not what I'm going to need to survive and thrive.

When someone asks something of me, it's very easy for me to decide whether I'm going do it or not based on priorities. For example, I heard somebody say that when it comes to travel, as a person who's married and has kids, they try never to be away from home overnight more than three days in two months. Period. When I first got married, my wife was a management consultant. She would leave on Monday and come back on Friday morning. It was really rough for us as a newly married couple. Now that we're more established and we have more control over our schedule, we're able to arrange our travel and work schedules to better respect our priorities. That's what it means to pay attention to the ABCs.

You can do the same thing. Ask yourself what your priorities are. What's vital? What's important? What's only nice? If you can sort your priorities into these categories, you'll have taken the first step toward being able to plan for success.

The MITs

In his book *Zen Habits: Handbook for Life*, author Leo Babauta talks about MITs. MITs are your Most Important Tasks. Each day, I'm trying to accomplish at least three tasks.[12] They are not in the vital category, because the vitals are going to get done. They're more in the realm of the important and the nice. The work I do as an author, as a podcaster, and as a blogger are all these kinds of tasks.

21

I try to make sure that I schedule my entire week and literally put down on a calendar what I'm going to do. My goal is to make sure it's no more than three things on any given day. If I can accomplish those three things, awesome.

Most people do very little because they have too much on their plate. To avoid this problem, I've learned that *planning* is vital for me. It's in my A column. Every morning, I'm up early. I'm taking care of those core things, and planning is one of the core things. And then the MIT comes out of that planning session, and I put it on my calendar. I put things on timers, so timers go off to remind me to do X, Y, and Z. It helps a whole lot, because knowing your ABCs, knowing your MITs, makes it possible to sort through everything you might be doing on any given day and focus on the things that are most important.

Proper Planning Prevents Poor Performance

When I have not done well getting ready for a class, it's because of poor planning. When I fail at something, I always ask myself whether better planning could have prevented that failure, and I try to figure out how to plan better next time.

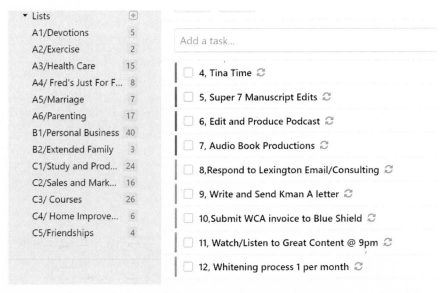

Figure 8 AbCs on the left and the MTs on the right Photo Courtesy of Fred Opie

If you can do these things early in the morning, you're going to be able to accomplish a whole lot more. And when you have a task and you can check something off, you get the same type of adrenaline rush you get when you eat chocolate. It makes you feel good. I teach my kids about this sense of accomplishment, which is a great way to generate positive feelings throughout the day without losing sight of the most important priorities in your life.

» Proper planning prevents poor performances.

» Planning carefully is planning to win.

» Falling in love requires a pulse; staying married for life requires a plan.

CHAPTER 4

Preparation

Planning is important, but it's only one part of preparation. *Preparation* means simply getting ready for whatever it is that you want to do successfully—whether that's a theater performance, an instrumental recital, a sports game, or something else. When you're going to pitch to somebody, be it pitching yourself or pitching a product or service, you've got to prepare if you want to knock it out of the ballpark. That's why the fourth principle of the Super Seven is preparation: what it means, how to do it, and how it helps prepare us for success.

A Key to Self-Confidence

Preparation is an important key to self-confidence. You can't have confidence that you're going to do well if you didn't put in the time to prepare. Let me talk about the dialectic of stress, or of being nervous, for a minute: stress reminds us that we need to prepare, and after we have done the proper amount of work, our confidence increases and the stress decreases.

Figure 9 Paul Robeson as Othello. Robeson was an All American football player at Rutgers University, an actor, superb singer, and an activist, Courtesy of the New York Public Library

If you're feeling really stressed out when you do things, stop and ask yourself, "How much time did I put into preparing?" When I have not properly prepared, I get stressed out. I teach a number of classes, and before every class, I am a little nervous. I let nervous become normal, because I've realized that when I haven't been a little bit nervous, I haven't taken that particular class seriously enough, and I didn't prepare well. It didn't turn out well. The same thing is true in sports: right before a game starts, you feel a little bit of the stress and get yourself a little bit fired up. I have found that to be good, because it means I'm taking the game seriously. Prepare for the worst, because the best-case scenarios don't require preparation.

Here is an additional thought on the idea of proper preparation: in her research, Carol Dweck found that you cannot be in the zone and turn your ability on and off without proper preparation. What is proper preparation? Working hard, keeping one's focus, and intensely stretching yourself to become better than your ordinary ability or your gift. Proper preparation is working your hardest to become your best you when it's time to perform.[13]

You Don't Need to Prepare for Something Good to Happen

You don't need to prepare for something that's going to be good. You have to prepare for the inevitability that something might not go well. Recently, when I was teaching, something went wrong with the technology, and we had to reboot the computer twice. We lost probably about twenty minutes total. What did I do? Before the next class, I went over to the experts on the software we're using and covered everything. By doing that, I prepared for the worst. But what if I hadn't done that? I wouldn't have had confidence that the class would go well.

This isn't an attitude of pessimism. I don't want you to think "Prepare for the worst" is being pessimistic. But the bottom line is, if things are really going to go well, you don't need to prepare for that. You need to prepare for the possibility of something not going well.

Prepare in Advance

Whatever you can do a month in advance, prepare to do it. I am a writer, an entrepreneur, a parent, an athlete—we all wear so many different hats in life. But if you can prepare in advance, it helps you. If I know that on the twenty-fourth of the month, I have something planned, I don't want to wait until the twenty-third to get everything lined up. I want to back it out. I put it on my calendar. I'll put a timer on my calendar, and I have an alarm go off two weeks before. Then I'll have another notification go off a week before, and another maybe two days before. That way, I don't have to think about it. When those reminders go off, then I dedicate some time to that task. I find it makes my life a whole lot easier.

Some people say they work better under stress. I tell people, "If you work better under stress, give yourself a false deadline." Or, if you have to deliver something to another person, ask them to give you an early delivery date. If working a month in advance isn't going to help you, start working a week in advance instead of the night before it's due.

Check the Weather

I have an example that will hit this home. The first time I ever went to Chicago was about five years ago, and I did not check the weather. It was October. I got off the plane, and it was the coldest weather. Now, keep in mind, folks, I went to Syracuse University for undergrad and graduate school. Syracuse is cold. Chicago was cold on steroids the October I went there, and I did not check the weather. I dressed for an October in New England, and, oh, did I suffer. Have you ever been so cold that no matter what you do, you can't get warm? That's what it felt like.

A year or two later, I had another trip to Chicago. This is Chicago in April, and anybody who's ever spent any time in Chicago will tell you it can be really cold in April. I said, "All right, this is not going to happen to me again. I'm going to be prepared." So I had a pair of long-johns on. You ever see those old movies where you see cowboys wearing the full-length long-johns? They're red. They have buttons on the crotch for if you have to go to the bathroom, and believe me, it's not easy if you have to go to the bathroom quick. But I had that on underneath this suit I was wearing, and I had a winter coat in my hand, and I got off of the plane, again not having checked the temperature. That particular April, it was like 85, 90 degrees, and from the minute I got off that plane, I started dripping sweat. I had to take public transportation all the way to my hotel, and I was just literally like a walking sauna. And I was saying, "Oh my gosh, this is so stupid. How did I do this? How did I do this?"

27

A year later, I had to go to Chicago. And this brainiac finally realized, "Maybe you should check the weather?" So I checked the weather. I dressed appropriately, and the time I spent in Chicago was light years better than the two previous experiences, simply by preparing for that trip.

It's Better to Look Ahead and Prepare Than to Look Back and Regret

Now here's a quote from Jackie Joyner Kersee, who was an Olympian: "It's better to look ahead and prepare than to look back and regret."

Particularly in track and field, if you turn and look behind, you can literally lose seconds off of your speed and then lose the race. So it's better to look ahead and prepare. Keep focused on looking out of the windshield instead of in the rearview mirror. You don't want to be one of those people who, fifteen or twenty years down the road, talks about "shoulda, coulda, woulda." My mother used to say that all the time! "Don't give me one of those, 'shoulda, coulda, wouldas.' Do it ahead of time."

There Are No Secrets To Success

> *"There are no secrets to success. Success is the result of preparation, hard work, and learning from failure."*
>
> **—Colin Powell**

If you do something well, don't just think it's a one-off. Stop and analyze what you did well. Why did that pitch go so well to that company or that organization that you've been trying to get in the door with? Think about why you were successful, and don't let it be one of those, "I don't know." Think about it! If you can learn from it, it could be a formula you use to be even more successful in the future.

Napoleon Hill made important contributions in the personal growth field as an author and speaker. He says, "Hope is the outcome of preparation, yours or somebody else's." That is deep. Hope is the outcome of preparation. The more you prepare, the more hope you have. I think we're quite aware of the fact that when you don't have hope, that's when your emotions can get out of whack. It's when you can get very depressed, when you can get very down. But preparation gives you great hope that you will have some success. I love that one particularly.

Satchel Paige was an outstanding pitcher in the old Negro Leagues before African Americans were allowed into Major League baseball in this country. He later went on to pitch in the Major Leagues in his forties. He spent a lot of time pitching in different parts of the Caribbean, including the Dominican Republic, Cuba, and Puerto Rico. He said, "Prepare now to do the kind of work that you'll love, and you'll never have a job later." That is an outstanding thought, that if you put in the time now, you'll be able to do the work you love, and it won't even feel like a job.

Another way to put that is, "Have your vocation feel like a vacation." If you prepare well, you can do that. In order for me to become a college professor, I had to do intense preparation. I had to get an undergraduate degree—four years of time and expense. I had to get a master's degree—another two to three years—and then I had to get a PhD. On average, most people will complete a PhD, if you're on a fast track, in five years. For me, it took almost nine years. That's a lot of preparation. However, the options it gives me now to do actually what I want to do are amazing. Every time I teach, does it go perfectly? No. But I'd say 80 percent of the time, I'm actually having a blast. When I'm grading papers, do I love it? No. But every other part of being a professor has been more than I thought it would be. The opportunities in the classroom and out of the classroom have made it wonderful.

Or, to take another example, I've played in two national championships, and we lost both times to the same team, John Hopkins University. I later interviewed many of those players from John Hopkins, and they told me that on Monday morning before the championship game, they got a scouting report on my team. It was a very thick report. In addition, they had films. So they knew the tendency of our team. They knew what to look for ahead of time, and because of that, they didn't just beat us—they *destroyed* us in both national championships. I think they beat us so bad because they were prepared.

What kind of scouting reports have you created for the industry or career you want to enter? Do you know the person you want to work for? You can learn a lot about a person if they're on Instagram or from their Twitter feed. Sometimes it's not just what they're tweeting but also who they are following. You can look on YouTube. Have they been interviewed? Knowing what to focus on is essential. If you're going into a company, there are many people you could meet, but who are the key people who you want to know who they are? What makes them tick?

As an educator, I must share this closing thought from the work of Carol Dweck: if you are a teacher, coach or leader, it's important that you give equal preparation time and attention to all of your students, players, or team members, regardless of their starting ability.[14]

Some things you might consider preparing the night before:

» Lunch bag, particularly if you want to eat better

» Bag with exercise gear

» Bag with work necessities

» Wardrobe

» Overnight bag for a trip

» Snow blower, shovels, gear before a storm

CHAPTER 5

Management

Managing Time

Be careful of time-jackers.

—Darrell Jones

The late Episcopal pastor John Cherry developed seven principles that have been integral to my life. You may be an atheist, or you may have a concept of god or the supernatural that's very different from mine, but just consider this: Organization is God's plan to simplify your life.

There's two things we want to cover when we talk about this principle. Number one is how you organize and arrange your time. I met a man just the other day who has it in his heart to write a book, and what's keeping him from doing it is that he's terrified. When I think about fear, the acronym I use is "False Evidence Appearing Real," which is a way of understanding that most of the stuff you are scared of will never come to pass. And it helps if you can organize your time, because often fear comes from a lack of organization.

Finish What You Start or Cut Your Losses and Move On

All of the books I have published have started with just a concept, an idea. I make time in my schedule to open a file on my computer, and I give it some title that might be what ends up being the final title, or it might change. Then, anything related to that idea, whether it be a podcast, an article from a newspaper, or a quote, I start throwing into that particular file. From that file, I make time to start producing blog posts, which is one of the reasons why I teach blogging as an important way to learn how to write well. If I have enough to blog for a considerable length of time, I can then take those blog posts and put them into a Word document. Then I make time in my schedule to expand each idea from just a blog post to a part of a chapter, and then to a chapter, and then to a number of chapters. Over time, I have seven chapters, or eight chapters—and I have a book. But it all comes from organizing your time and things.

Before you decide to acquire something, ask yourself, "Do I have the time to maintain it?" I want you to think about that. Do you have the time to maintain it? I try to only take in things that I know I have time to maintain. As a matter of fact, when I buy new clothing, I make sure I take that same amount of clothing out of my closet, because I find that the less I have, the more time I have to maintain it. That's time management. That's what we're talking about, managing your time. For example, if you're going to get a new car, ask yourself, "Do I have the time to maintain it?" If you're going to start a graduate program, ask, "Do I have the time to do the work necessary to finish the degree requirements?" A lot of people start. A lot of people don't finish, because they don't think about the time commitment necessary to do so.

Another guy I met recently, Darrel Jones, is an absolutely fascinating person. He spent thirty-two years in jail for a crime he did not commit. He said, "Do you know what a time-jacker is? When you are dealing with someone who is keeping you from more important things—your family, your priorities, whatever it is—they are time-jackers, and you have to be careful of time-jackers." What he had learned to value more than anything else, as an incarcerated person, was time, because you can never get it back. If you knew somebody was carrying an infectious disease and they were coming toward you, you would clear out. But we all know someone who's a time-jacker, yet we allow them to come in and jack more time from us—the very same way somebody would jack your car at a stoplight and take it from you. You can't afford to allow that to happen.

Figure 10 Malcolm X 1964, Courtesy of Library of Congress

Respect for Time Determines Success or Failure

> *"In all of your deeds, the proper value and respect for time determines success or failure"*
>
> **–Malcolm X**

Success and failure are both planned events. So here's Malcolm saying, in all of your deeds, in everything you do, the proper value and respect you have for time determines both success or failure. Doing what's not important merely uses up your time. Remember when we covered planning, understanding your vitals, and your ABCs, I said that you have to have priorities, and then I talked about knowing what your MITs are, your Most Important Tasks. You can't afford to waste time.

Folks, at the time of writing this book I am fifty-five years old. Time is urgent for me. Why? Because how many people do you see who are doing some of the things on my bucket list that require all kinds of energy and vigor? Some of the things on my bucket list you can't do at age seventy. You can't do at age eighty. You have to do them now, while you have the health. You can't afford to be messing around, wasting your time. When the time to perform arrives, the time to prepare has passed. This is super important: you have to pay attention to how much time you have left to prepare for something. That's why you can't let anybody time-jack you.

When you are under thirty, or even under fifty, it can be harder to see the importance of this point, but as you get older, time begins to have a greater value. I don't say this to be morbid. You simply come to understand how important time is, and that you can't waste it.

Calendar Cushions

Let's talk about the idea of "calendar cushions" to reduce chaos. My day started at the early hour of 4:30 a.m. I like to make sure I get six and half to seven hours of sleep. So I start out early in the day with prayer at 4:30, followed by devotional time at 5:00. These early things I do are in my calendar, and they're repeated, so it's not like every day I'm opening up my calendar and plugging this stuff in. I put it in one time, and I set it up to keep repeating every day.

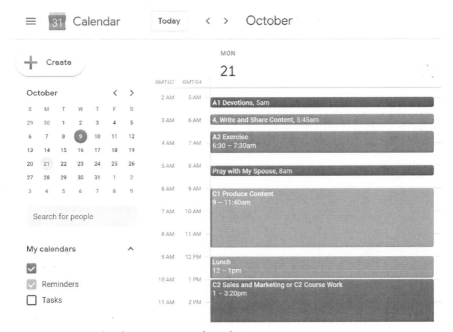

Figure 11 Calendar, Courtesy of Fred Opie

Then I get to 8:00, when I had a meeting with the guy who is my coach, so that's something I already plugged in. We had our coaching session. That lasted fifty minutes, and then we programmed immediately, saying, "Look, when's the next time I can talk with you?" I need this guy in my life. He helps me manage my time, my will, my emotions, my writing projects— all those different things that I have plugged into my calendar. I have my calendar color-coded so I can remember what I need to do in different categories, and then I set an alarm. The alarm goes off, telling me, "Hey, it's time for you to start reading and getting ready for class." Then I have the class.

Now, if it wasn't a day when I was teaching, I might have an event coded purple. Why purple? That was the color my wife picked for our wedding. So when I see that, I think of family, and for me, sitting down and being home for a family meal is critically important. My wife really helps me keep my life together.

Turning to the idea of "calendar cushions," I try to add a little time between things. For example, I know my daughter gets off the bus at 2:30, so I want to make sure I leave my office no later than, say, 1:50 to get there in time. I want to add that cushion on the calendar rather than say, "All right, she gets there at 2:30. I'll wind up and start heading home at 2:15." That's not enough cushion. It's going to create chaos.

When I'm late for something, I'm disrespecting your time. I'm saying, "You're not important. I'm more important. I'm the man. I'm more important. Therefore, you should wait." And I had enough experiences that caused me to really realize I was doing this, how arrogant that attitude was, before I made a change in my behaviors.

You might be busy, but are you effective? Just because you're busy doesn't mean you're effective. Thinking about how you spend the limited resource of your time—what you decide to do with it and who you decide to give it to—is an important step toward living your best life.

Managing People

When it comes to managing people, focus on helping others grow, mentoring, praising great effort, and encouraging collaboration among your team members. Great managers reward collaboration, teamwork, and hard work. They are also truth tellers and focus on keeping morale high. They are people full of gratitude for their team members and their contributions. Managers with a growth mindset, according to Carol Dweck, are leaders committed to growing, developing, training, coaching, and recognizing improvement. They also encourage critiques and dissent. Growth mindset managers are enthusiastic about teaching, learning, and giving and receiving feedback. Remember, managers are leaders, and leaders need to be readers dedicated to developing. Growth mindset managers understand that leaders are developed and not born. If you create an organization that champions training and learning, you will organically grow leaders among the ranks of your team.[15]

Relationships and Time

If you're in a friendship, you have to evaluate it: is this a win-win friendship? If you're in a relationship with people who are just constantly taking from you, it's not a relationship you want to maintain.

There are friendships, and then there are associations. What's the difference? Friendships are people who give to me, and I give to them, so that when I leave my time with them, I feel nourished and replenished. But sometimes people who you think are your friends suck you dry of all of who you are and all the energy you bring. You want to be in relationships that are mutually beneficial and that make you feel replenished.

What's an associate? An associate is someone who I will keep in touch with. They'll stay within my network. But they're not a friend. My friends are about four to five people who, when the stuff hits the fan, they seek me out, and they are here for me, and they help me get out of my problem. Your friends are the people who will carry your casket when you die. How many people do you really know like that? Or how many people are just kind of hanging on to you?

In the most practical sense, it's important to feed your relationships and friendships. For example, I make a plan every week to date my wife. I'm never going to stop dating my wife. Every Friday's a date day. We carve it out, and it takes something really important for us to allow anyone to steal that block of time away from us.

The same thing is true with my friends. I schedule time. I know a lot of guys, a lot of women, they'll have a weekend with their friends. One of my colleagues every year has a weekend with friends who go all the way back to college. He's now in his fifties. Planning time to be able to spend with your friends is important.

When you're doing something that's really important, like spending time with your primary relationship or your friends, you have to be there, not somewhere else. One of the ways you can be there when you're with your friends is to turn off your phone. Make sure you don't have your apps open and all these reminders going off. My wife will tell you, I'm notorious for having my phone going all the time. But when I go to bed, I turn off the ringer on my phone. I put it on airplane mode. I don't know how many years I've had a cell phone—twenty, twenty-five years now—and I've never missed an emergency. Whereas, if I leave the phone on with the Internet enabled, it's so easy for me to go to check out my Twitter feed, and the next thing I know it's an hour past my bedtime. That's why I have to discipline myself. Say to yourself, "Look, at 6:00, 8:00, 10:00"—whatever works for you—"I turn my phone off and put it on airplane mode, or I put it away."

Next time you go into a restaurant to eat, notice the number of people who aren't even interacting with each other. They're just looking at their smartphones. So one of the things that my wife and I will do, particularly on our dates or when we're out with the family, is leave our phones in the car, because it is so addictive and so easy to get distracted. That's one of the toughest time-jackers to deal with right now. We have everything from

Netflix to ESPN on the phone, and you have to be deliberate in order to keep yourself from being sucked into it.

Our time on earth is limited, and so we have to be intentional about how we choose to spend every minute and every hour that we have. Avoid time-jackers and invest your time in the people in your life who you love and care about. Invest your time in working on your ABCs and MITs. If you do so, before you know it, you will accomplish the important goals you set for your life.

CHAPTER 6
Learning Styles

"You haven't learned anything until you can take action and use it." That's Miami Dolphins head coach and Hall of Famer Don Shula and author Ken Blanchard. Research on learning styles shows that each and every one of us learns differently, and understanding how you learn can make a huge difference in advancing your goals. It also can help you learn how to share your point or pitch it to someone else. When you understand the best way to get something across to the person you're talking to, you are at a definite advantage.

The Five Learning Styles

There are five different learning styles: auditory learners, visual learners, kinesthetic learners (kinesiology is touch), analytical learners, and global learners. I'm going to unpack each of these and talk about them.

First, though, I should mention that most of us have a primary learning style as well as a secondary one. So you might find yourself in more than one of these descriptions.

Let's start with auditory learners. Auditory learners learn best by hearing, especially hearing things for themselves. This is me: I learn by taking information in and listening. I'm the kind of person who, when I'm at a presentation and other people might not want to ask questions, I'm asking those questions, because that's how I learn.

Then there are visual learners. For visual learners, watching and observing helps them learn. I had a student in a class who would make cartoons out of the content I shared. She drew absolutely phenomenal cartoons, but maybe you like to create diagrams, draw charts—anything visual. Visual learning might be a secondary style for me, because often when I'm at events I will find myself doodling what's being conveyed to me.

The kinesthetic learner is a person who might seem very ADHD, because movement and touch are very important for kinesthetic learners. Music is often helpful to them, as well. As an instructor, to help kinesthetic learners, I try to come up with a way to make the material more tactile so that they can better understand what I'm trying to get across.

The last two types of learners come from Herman Witkin's theory of how people process information.[16] While everyone has a learning style, whether that be auditory or visual or kinesthetic, there is also processing— how we get the information in our heads, move it around, and retain it. Witkin talked about the analytical learner and the global learner. Knowing which one you are might give you a better sense of who you are and how you think, or it might give you insight into people in your life who you work with, family members, or friends.

Let's begin with the analytical learner. Studies show that 50 percent of us are analytical learners, which means we learn better with specifics. "Give me an example," an analytical learner will say. I find myself doing that; sometimes I do it just to clarify. If someone writes a general concept, I'll be interested, but I'll say, "Give me an example to clarify it." The person who needs details might come off to someone else like a pain in the butt, but they're just trying to understand and make sense of what's going on. My wife is a visual analytical learner. She is a person who, when she's driving, she needs to have the GPS on to best analyze and process how to get from point A to B. She's a visual learner, obviously, because she likes to see where she's going. For me, I can look at a visual map, get it in my mind, and keep it in my mind, and it might not be necessary for me to actually see the visual again. Often, when I've driven to a place more than one time, I don't need to use the GPS anymore.

If you want to get across to an analytical learner, you have to break down what you're teaching or telling them about into bite-sized pieces. They're going to get the point you're trying to make a whole lot more easily that way. When we blog, some people will get the point with an image. Other people will get it through the narration and content, and still other people through the related hyperlinks. So we give people three different ways to consume what we're trying to get across to them.

Compared to the analytical learner, the global, or intuitive, learner is someone who learns better with the *context* clarified. On the bottom of every email I send, it says, "Context is just as important as content." Have you included the context for what you're trying to say? People who aren't global learners can be irritated when you give them too much information. They got it, they understand it, they're ready to go. But global learners need context.

It's the global learners who will constantly come back and ask questions, and these are different from the questions analytical learners ask. An analytical learner will say, "Give me an example." A global learner will learn better when they know *why* a topic is important. These are the people who are asking the "Why?" question. You have to answer the "Why?" question for a global learner if you want to get through to them. If you're going to pitch to a global learner, you have to give them the big picture. Once you give them the big picture, they're more receptive to the other parts of the story you're trying to share.

Half of us are analytical learners. Half of us are global learners. There's no right or wrong in this; there's just difference. Some of us have a dominant and a recessive learning style, which might mean we're asking both kinds of questions in different situations. That's not uncommon at all. But knowing what kind of learner you are means you can set up a process to help yourself learn better.

In his book *Rise and Grind*, Damon John from *Shark Tank* reveals for the first time that he's severely dyslexic, and he never knew it. Not only does it he talk about his own dyslexia, but he also says that he did research and found out some of the most noted entrepreneurs in history, like Richard Branson, are also dyslexic. Part of John's point is that the way God has wired your mind might come with disadvantages, but it will have major advantages, too. Dyslexia is not just a burden, it's also a blessing. You have to learn the way it works for you.

If you're a college student, you might take your learning style into account when you're choosing classes. How does the professor present? For an auditory learner, sometimes taking notes eliminates our ability to listen and process. But a kinesthetic learner needs the movement; that motion of writing helps you learn. You have to learn the way that works for you.

Analytical learners do better with specifics, with details. We learn better when the content is broken into steps. But the global or intuitive learner processes the information better with the context clarified, with knowing the *why*.

If you pay attention to your own experiences, you'll figure out what your learning style is. Just look for examples in your own life. What about when you are playing sports? Do you find you obtain information better from your coaches or from your teammates? Do you learn better from verbal instructions, a visual chart, a drill? Keep investigating, and you'll definitely figure out your learning style over time.

So why is knowing your learning style one of my Super Seven? Because in my own experience, it wasn't until I understood that I wasn't lazy, crazy, or stupid, but that I had a different learning style, that things began to turn around for me. And I'm convinced that the same is true for others. When you begin to study yourself the same way you would study everything necessary to purchase the right car or home, you will see a positive difference. I would even go as far to say that until you become introspective, you are going to cap what you are able to accomplish in your life. Why? Because earners must be learners, and leaders are learners. When you earn more, you can give more to causes greater than you, and when you lead with the right attitude, you can have a greater positive impact on the world around you.

CHAPTER 7
Leveraging Technology

The final Super Seven Principle is about how to leverage technology to help you achieve your goals. I include this principle because I think we tend to underestimate how many free tools are available that can help us be our best. What I've come to understand is that just like when playing jazz or cooking, with technology you have to know how to be improvisational. There's no rule that says that you have to use technology the way its designer created it to be used. I say no—instead, take advantage of all creations, including software, for your needs and goals and in the way that works best for you.

Google Contacts, Docs, and Hangouts

Let's look at how I use Google Contacts. (Google, you should be sending me a royalty for this.) I take my contacts, and instead of putting somebody's name, their phone number, and their email in, with additionally maybe their website or a link to their profile, I will put in the courses that I am actually teaching as contacts. I can find all my courses easily in my contacts, and I keep in those contacts the essential information for that course: how to get to the Blackboard site that I'm using for the class, Webex if I'm teaching online, all of the related Google links for the books I'm using in the class, any YouTube videos I want to share during a class. If there are images that I have links to, they'll be hot-linked in there. In the notes area, where you can actually write different things, I will often take attendance. I'll put my workgroups there. By putting my courses in as contacts, everything I need is at my fingertips.

HSS2019 Food and Politics (TR 8:00 AM and 9:45AM)

Courses

http://www.kcrw.com/news-culture/shows/good-food • Nixon/Food 8:42

https://www.youtube.com/watch?v=3Km-LGZHh20 • Dick Gregory 1968 start at 16:12

https://www.youtube.com/watch?v=a2MR5XbJtXU • Public Speaking

http://site.ebrary.com/lib/babson/m . • Upsetting the Apple cart

https://www.wnyc.org/series/the-eights • Profile

Attendance:
*Grading:
Proactive Learning:

Figure 12 An example of one of my courses formatted in my contacts, Courtesy of Fred Opie

Not only do I do that with the courses I teach, but when I'm writing a book, I will create a contact for the book. That contact entry becomes an easy way for me to work on the book project as life is going on. What do I mean by that? If I'm traveling and I have some time to do some work while I'm waiting to get on the train, the plane, or whatever it is, I can go to that contact and access some of the information.

I do the same thing with Google Docs. I will have one for anything I'm working on. Most recently, I had the opportunity to go to a local prison and teach, so I created a Google Doc titled "Prison Visit," and all the information, the notes about what I was going to teach, the agenda for that particular meeting—it's all in the same place.

To take another example, I was listening to a podcast about how to improve your marriage. There is a new book out by Les and Leslie Parrott called *Making Marriage Happy*. The Parrotts say that it's your job to make your own marriage happy, and one of the six strategies that they suggest is to come up with a bucket list between you and your significant other of fifty things you want to do together. So my wife and I created a Google Doc where we started putting down all of these wish-list items. One of the ones we have on there is a vacation in Paris, another is to travel across the country by train with a train pass that will allow you to stop at any city you want, and another is to go cross-country in an RV. There are a lot of different things on the bucket list. A Google Doc is a great way to organize that kind of information.

There's also Google Hangouts. A lot of the meetings I do with my research assistants and graduate assistants, or committees I volunteer with, I'll do as a Google Hangout. There's a lot of meeting technology that saves time by making it so you don't have to meet in person. It's worthwhile to get familiar with this kind of technology.

Social Media

A lot of people do not leverage social media enough for their business purposes. Social media isn't just about putting fun or foolish things out there. It gives you tools to create community and networking toward your personal goals. For example, I use Instagram as a marketing device. There's so much you can do with Instagram, not only to share with family and friends, but also to share with people who you want to meet in the marketplace, people who you want to know about what you're doing. When I do my weekly podcast, I take a screenshot of the podcast for that week, and I share it on Instagram. I also will share the same thing on Facebook. I'll share it via Twitter. Twitter is awesome if you're trying to get hold of someone or get on their radar, or even if you just want to learn a little bit more about them.

There are a few important things to think about when it comes to using social media effectively. First, when you're using social media, you have to know how to make your images appear the way you want them to look. Recently, a young man won an award, and someone tagged me on the award on Twitter. I took a look at this young man's profile. He was being recruited as a student athlete, but the image he was using for his profile was not the kind of image that projected the qualities I was looking for in a student athlete or leader. That's not a smart thing to do.

Or, to take another example, I had a guest on my podcast, and I went to their Facebook page. There, I found all these images of the person with alcoholic drinks in their hand. These were images of partying, but this person's Facebook page was set so anybody could access it. Is that the image that you want to present to the world?

You also have to keep your social media accounts and images up to date. Make sure you take the highest-quality photo possible when you're sharing it as your profile image. These are just really important things that people don't necessarily think about.

Pinterest is another great technology. Any time I post something new on my blog, I make sure that when I set it up, it's connected to all my social media, so all I have to do is press one button when I publish a new post. The image will go to Pinterest, and it will update on my Facebook page. It'll update on Twitter, and it will update on Instagram. It's really easy.

The other nice thing about the blog platform that Square and Wordpress use is that you can time-release any of this stuff, so I can drip out one day at a time whatever I want. I can be out of town and not available to do blogging every day, but I'm able to set up the platform to publish three or four different posts, and then each post will release to all the different social media platforms, like Twitter and Facebook.

The last social media technology I want to highlight is LinkedIn. LinkedIn allows you to connect with people and let them know about what you're doing. If you are going to be holding a meet-up, you can let people know about it on LinkedIn—and it's probably worth it for you to pay the little bit more additional fee they charge so that you can have the opportunity to do more things on LinkedIn. Facebook and LinkedIn are awesome ways to connect with people, to establish your brand, and to get your brand out there.

So I would encourage you to move beyond using social media platforms only to connect with friends and family. You do not need to have a whole lot of money, or to borrow any money, to launch a company when you have all these free platforms at your fingertips. Finally, remember that there are people who don't have your best interests at heart, so you want to be careful how much you share.

Making the Most of Social Media Networks

If you want to establish an expertise and make a name for yourself, you can do it through social media. The best way to get interviewed by an outlet like the *New York Times* or to get on the radio is to find out who the producer or editor is, or who the beat writer is, and then begin to follow them on social media and compliment them on their stories. When you compliment them, you'll begin to get their attention, and then you can actually pitch ideas you'd like to write or be an expert on: "Have you thought about doing a story on X, Y, and Z?" You can use the technology and open a free blog to start, creating an expertise for yourself.

The same thing is true for a podcast. Your smartphone is more than enough for you to record a high-quality audio file about something you're interested in. You can publish a podcast, whether it's once a week, once a month, once a quarter. When you do this, you're drawing not only on the technology but also on your own existing networks. To take myself as an example, I have the lacrosse tribe. I have the tribe of historians, who write and work in the area of food history and food culture. I have the podcasting community. All those communities are networks, and when you have those networks, they're a resource to go to when you're trying to accomplish something. Within those tribes, you already have a certain level of credibility and a relationship. So you draw on your existing network in order to start up a conversation with someone via social media, LinkedIn, Facebook, or whatever.

Often, when I'm trying to get a guest to come on my show, I'll reach out to them via Facebook. I think the most important thing to remember in these conversations is that you're not just reaching out in order to take something from the person. You also want to find out what can you do to help this person—maybe by introducing them to someone in your network, maybe some other way. But you always want to be leveraging technology to propose a win-win situation to the person you're reaching out to, not just a situation where you're asking to be given something.

Budgeting Tool

I highly recommend an app called EveryDollar, which is at everydollar.com. You can download it on an iPhone, Android, and on your desktop. It's what my wife and I use to manage every dollar. It's awesome. You put your income in for that month at the top, and then you start plugging in your expenses, whether it's housing, gas, groceries, major expenses, all the way down to fun money—a certain amount of money for fun, entertainment, travel. When you know your fun money budget, and you use an app like EveryDollar to track it, you can go out on a date with cash in an envelope and pay cash for your entertainment with no sense of guilt at all, because the expense is budgeted. I highly recommend using EveryDollar or a similar app or service to keep track of your budget in this way.

Make Technology Work for You

Leveraging Technology is a Super Seven because it gives you the ability to do more than you can naturally do without it. I see technology, when used correctly, like a superpower: it gives you the ability to supernaturally organize yourself and as a result simplify your life. It also gives you the ability to supernaturally communicate with influencers who are ordinarily unavailable. With the use of Twitter, Facebook, or Instagram, you can have one-on-one communication with some of the most important people in the world.

Many of you reading this are like some of my friends: they're proud to say that when it comes to technology, they are dinosaurs. But consider the fact that if you do not keep up with the latest and greatest technology, you're going to get left behind. In addition, consider the fact that every time I learn new technology, I have effectively inoculated myself against dementia or another memory-related mental health disorder. People who are learning and developing, studies show, are less likely to suffer from these debilitating mental health and aging problems.

I know learning curves can suck. We have all had the experience of getting a new cell phone and leaving it in the package until we were forced to learn it, and then, after we learned how to use the new phone, wishing we had started using it months earlier. I implore you, don't be that person. (I confess, I have been that person more often than I care to admit.)

When it comes to selecting technology, here are my suggestions: ask tech-savvy family and friends what they are using. Read the advice in industry blogs and magazines. Finally, listen to what the tech experts recommend who come on your favorite shows. For example, I like the suggestions of tech expert Russell Holly of *Android Central*. He's a regular on Tech Tuesday on *All Sides with Host Ann Fisher* on WOSU FM. I listen to this Ohio show and others like it as a podcast on my smartphone.

CONCLUSION

Let's review the most important parts of each of the Super Seven, starting with **evaluation**. In any area of our lives, we need clear and honest understanding of where we are so we can move forward. You must be honest about your ability to take and give constructive feedback. I define "constructive feedback" as giving people the information they need to make course corrections as they journey through life. How can I be better at giving constructive feedback so I help those I parent, coach, teach, and lead?

We all need to be intentional about knowing how to evaluate and give feedback to the different people in our sphere of influence. Remember that we learn more from failure than success, so don't freak out when you come up short when being evaluated. Second, remember that an evaluation lets us know where we stand in order to improve our standing. Every time we get up in the morning, we stand in front of a bathroom mirror in order to learn how we stand in terms of our hygiene—at least I hope you do! A balanced and healthy desire to be evaluated is a good thing.

Do be cognizant, though, of the person whose authority you are submitting to. Here are a couple principles that will help you in terms of discerning if that person is evaluating you with your best interests at heart. Do they care about you? People who care about you will tell you the truth even when it hurts. Do they love themselves? If a person is not confident and doesn't love themselves, their evaluation might be more destructive than constructive. Here, it helps to remember the saying, "Hurt people hurt people." If someone is evaluating you from a position of low self-esteem and hurt, I wouldn't trust their evaluation. Remember, too, the principle of agreement: If one person gives you a poor evaluation, take it with a grain of salt. However, if you get that same evaluation from several people who know you, care about you, and who you trust, then you need to listen to their feedback. For example, when I am working on a new book project, I send out possible book covers to the people who I know and trust and solicit their feedback. I then move forward based on consensus. One of my favorite proverbs says there is wisdom in the multitude of counsel. What I am doing is obtaining the evaluation of several wise people, because it's a wise thing to do. If you are one of those people who does not have the ability to learn from feedback, you had better start working on that if you want to succeed in life.

Communication is our second Super Seven Principle. Now, communication does not come second because it's less important than evaluation. Each of the principles put together will make a difference in your life. If you have something hard to say to somebody in terms of feedback, focus on speaking the truth in love. In addition, if you cannot say something nice, do not say anything at all—especially if you know the person you are speaking to does not have thick skin. Pay attention to *when* you can assess the person or group you are communicating with. Solicit from them the best time and way to contact them. Be as positive as you can, remembering the ratio of sharing at least one positive attribute for every negative issue you may need to address. Consider when you are at your best and ask yourself, "Perhaps I should wait until tomorrow before reaching out to this person? Maybe I should schedule this speaking event earlier in the evening when I am at my best?" Similarly, remember the sandwich: open up the conversation with a positive, then slide in what might be hard for the person to hear, and then end the conversation with another positive thing to say.

The Super Seven Principle of Communication also reminds us to work on our public speaking and teaching. Remember the importance of brevity, and leverage silence to emphasize a point. Raise and lower your voice to underscore an idea. Think about your cadence, speaking not too fast or too slow. Remember that public speaking is an art form that you have to do over and repeatedly if you want to be good at it. Similarly, writing is a form of communication, in that it must be practiced in order to improve it. If you are like me and have a lot of typos as part of ADHD-related challenges, if a doctor has documented this behavioral health issue, you have the right to support, such as an editor to help with your writing. Studies show that if you want to write better, read more. If you want to speak better, start listening to recordings or podcasts of great speakers or consuming any media in which they share the secrets of the craft. In addition, for sure remember that good public speaking is a craft. Remember that we say things verbally and nonverbally. Ask your friends and loved ones about what you have been conveying nonverbally. If you do not like what you hear, be intentional about changing it. This will take time, but you can do it.

The principle of **planning** can be summarized by saying, "Don't forget your ABCs and your MITs." The bottom line with planning is getting organized, and organization is God's plan to simplify your life. If your life seems chaotic, there is a good chance that you have not taken the time to organize your time and/or your money. It could be that you need an organizing tool, such as a hard-copy or digital planning device. Know yourself well and then decide when is it best for you to plan your day: the night before or the morning of. Planning is about knowing yourself and knowing the people you work with or live with.

Planning is also about the principle of sowing and reaping, which is how we provide for ourselves. Every year, a farmer plans to plant a crop so that he or she can reap a harvest. When you plan to organize your schedule, you plan to have success in your life. If you show me somebody who has consistent, ongoing successful outcomes, I will show you an organized person. If you want to stop losing your keys, develop a plan to keep them in the same place every day. Plan good habits in your life and get good results. A team that wins a championship in many ways is not surprised when they achieve their goal. Why? Because months and years earlier, that team's coach or team captain worked out a mutually agreed-upon plan to achieve that outcome. Remember, the difference between a goal and a dream is that a goal has a detailed written plan that must be executed to make it come to pass.

Farmers know from experience that the more time they put into carefully planting their crops, the more they will harvest in the months to come. So it is with putting in quality **preparation** time. It is not easy for many people because they do not see a direct result between preparation and results in a society that wants same-day delivery of the things they desire. For example, in my case, it took months and years to write this book and consistently put the time into preparing the manuscript. However, I will not see the results for months or even years. That has been the case with other books that I have written. You prepare and prepare with the promise that something good will come out of the effort. It is a hard lesson for many people, and that's why they skimp on preparation. As a result, things do not go as well as they would like.

When I think about it, preparation and dedication to it requires accepting a great deal of delayed gratification. As I have heard one person say, long-term success requires a commitment to getting on the cover of *Slow Success* magazine. However, I cannot think of anything in my life in which success came quickly and without a lot of sacrifice. If you fall in love with the process, you will increasingly be able to embrace the principle of preparation—of doing the work necessary when nobody else is watching. A book full of many examples of what I am talking about is Chris Hogan's best-selling *Everyday Millionaire*. It is the largest US study of millionaires, for which interviews were done with ten thousand of them. What the study showed is that the overall majority of millionaires in this country are first-generation wealthy. That means they started out with little to nothing and plotted a course to becoming a millionaire: spending less than they earned the majority of their life, staying out of debt, consistently investing in good mutual funds or real estate after they got out of debt, and paying off their home mortgage in less than fifteen years. They did not wake up one day and say, "Wow, how did my net worth become a million or more dollars?" No, they are people who clearly understood the sacrifices and work it took to prepare to reach a million-dollar net worth. The degree to which you are willing to prepare will determine how much success you will enjoy in life.

In terms of the Super Seven Principle of **management**, there are two factors: managing yourself and managing others. When I think about management, I think about the principle of organization, which is God's plan to simplify our lives. To be our best, we need to know how much sleep we need and when we are most productive or in the zone, and we need to protect those times and to be aware of time-jackers. One of the hardest things about time management is learning to submit yourself to a calendar or other organizational tool, scheduling your day, and trying to create habits around things you do at the same time every day. Similarly, we have to submit ourselves to using timers on calendars to lock in a time commitment and then put it out of our minds until the alarm goes off hours, days, weeks, or months later. Calendars and other similar devices help protect our time so that we can be at our best and most productive.

Another thing to remember about time is to practice being in the present. That means turning off devices and focusing on the thing at hand. When you are at work, work, and when you're at home, be with family. That simple piece of advice goes a long way in managing your time. I find it particularly problematic when I am talking to somebody and they are distracted. You know what they say: We get irritated by the things that we have done to others. That is so true! And remember the farmer and the principle of sowing and reaping. Sow your time into good and healthy activities, and you will reap great rewards later.

In that regard, I'd also like to share my twenty-minute principle. I try to work in twenty-minute spurts of remaining focused on the activity or task at hand. I have learned over the years that twenty minutes of exercise goes a long way toward keeping you fit. Similarly, twenty minutes of reading or writing, committed to consistently over a long period of time, results in an article or book. Just focus on the twenty minutes in front of you with great intensity and commitment, and you'll be amazed at how much more productive you are. Think about that in your relationships with your loved ones as well. A twenty-minute walk every day can greatly improve your relationship with your spouse or children.

Another important aspect of time management is agreement. If you work with somebody, you need to let him or her know when you need your twenty minutes of undivided attention to work on something or to meet with them. The same is true about love: be in agreement about what you need.

In addition, keep in mind that you don't owe anyone an explanation for making a twenty-minute appointment to do something that you need to do, like relaxing. I let my family know that on Saturday and Sunday evenings during the football season, I plan to watch highlights of college and professional football. I think it is a better use of my time than watching a single game for two or three hours. Most of my male counterparts watch several games each Saturday and Sunday. I am not criticizing them; I am just telling you my strategy until the end-of-the-season playoff games are aired. I share my plans for this strategy for unwinding with my family so that we can be in agreement about what is going on, and nobody has unmet expectations.

In many ways, time management is agreeing to do the things you said you would do when you said you would do them. Similarly, smart goals have specific dates and times for their completion. Finally, consider getting up early in the morning before the rest of your family. Use that time to get in shape or start and complete writing the book you have always wanted to publish. I love taking advantage of the early morning and accomplishing more in the three hours between five and eight than most people accomplish all day.

Investing time in understanding your **learning style** is time well spent. You will be far more productive when you figure out what you need to wrap your mind around a learning curve. Consider all the dimensions involved in learning: the space you work in the best, the type of sound that works best for you, even if that means absolutely no sound at all. What about lighting, seating, surfaces to write on, whether they be hard copy or electronic platforms? In my case, I have been writing using Dragon software to dictate my writing for many years. I cannot imagine what it would be like to write without it.

What if you could explain to your loved ones and colleagues the easiest way for you to understand what they are trying to share with you? Think about how your frustration level would drastically decrease if you shared the things that trigger you or that make life easier for you in terms of learning. Some people need the visual, and some people need the explanation. We are all different, and it is not about who's smarter—it's about understanding difference and respecting it. It's amazing to me when I observe twins and listen to what their parents say about just how different they are. It is the same when you are a parent of two or more children, or when you are a coach; effective coaches and general managers have learned over time how to approach each player differently. And that comes with time, studying how different people respond to different situations and what they say they need. Remember that people communicate how they learn best in their verbal and nonverbal feedback. Pay attention and learn.

Finally, **leveraging technology** is something that I do, but not readily, because I hate the learning curve involved in becoming fluent with a new device. I say "fluent" because to me, learning a new device is like learning a foreign language. (I speak from my experience of learning Spanish while in graduate school.) As a podcaster, I use different technologies all the time, and sometimes I get depressed trying to troubleshoot problems that regularly come up. At the same time, I am amazed at just how intuitive and easy the most recent technological innovations are. For example, I was getting ready go to church on Sunday, and the temperature was crazy cold, about 30°F. So what we do is go outside and warm up the car so that when you put your bottom on those seats, it won't feel like a freezer. I recently bought a used pickup truck—something I've wanted to do for a while. I love the truck, but because it's an older model, I learned how easy it is to lock your keys in the truck with the engine running! I had to call our local police to come and use their gizmos—that's right, technology—to get me into my truck. Once the officer unlocked the door, my family headed off to our worship service. There, I shared the experience with another member of the church who recently bought a much nicer and newer pickup truck. He told me the technology in his truck makes it impossible for him to lock the keys in the cab. The automatic locking device has a program that prevents it from locking the car if the key is in the ignition. Now ain't that something? So I really recommend that you read magazines and listen to experts talk about the latest and greatest technology out there. After you have had a listen and learned about new technology, decide if it can help your life.

Do be aware, though, that every invention and technological innovation has both positive and negative aspects. Cell phones are great, but they are also great distractions. They keep people from being present. At the same time, how amazing they are—for example when you use the flashlight software at a time when you do not have a flashlight on hand. There are too many people in my age bracket, over fifty-five, who have decided to pack it in and not learn any new technology. They brag about being a dinosaur. Don't be a dinosaur. It's nothing to brag about.

If you made it this far in reading this book, and you put the Super Seven to work in your life, you are going to experience a greater quality of life at work and at home. I am not a smart guy, I'm just smart enough to learn from others and to learn from my mistakes. In my book *Start with Your Gift*, I share all the stupid mistakes I made as I moved from nineteen years old to having a fully developed frontal cortex. As I like to tell people, I paid the stupid tax, so you don't have to. Likewise, in this book I have tried to lay out all those times I have messed up and wasted time. We could have entitled this book, *Seven Ways to Do Things Better Than Fred Tried to Do Them the First Time*, lol.

I hang out on Instagram, Twitter, and Facebook. Connect with me and share the principles from this book that are helping you accomplish your goals with others.

Fred Opie
Winter 2019
Babson Park, Massachusetts

ABOUT THE AUTHOR

 r. Frederick Douglass Opie, is an author, college professor, podcaster, and coach. Opie has appeared in the *New York Times, Washington Post, Oprah Magazine* and on NPR, BBC Radio, the History Channel, and PBS television. He played lacrosse at Syracuse University and on a U.S. men's national team.

Other Published Works

Start With Your Gift: Understand And Monetize it While Serving Others With It (Opie Press)

Southern Food and Civil Rights: Feeding the Revolution (American Palate Series)

Zora Neale Hurston on Florida Food: Recipes, Remedies, and Simple Pleasures (American Palate Series)

Upsetting the Apple Cart: Black and Latino Coalitions in New York from Protest to Public Office (Columbia History of Urban Life Series, ed. Kenneth Jackson, Columbia University Press)

Black Labor Migration in Caribbean Guatemala, 1882-1923 (Florida Work in the Americas Series, University of Florida Press)

Hog and Hominy: Soul Food from Africa to America (Arts and Traditions of the Table: Perspectives on Culinary History Series, ed. Albert Sonnenfeld, Columbia University Press)

INDEX

ENDNOTES

1   Carol Dweck, *Mindset: The New Psychology of Success* (New York: Ballantine, 2016), pp. 18, 185, 221, 237.

2   John C. Maxwell, *Failing Forward: Turning Mistakes into Stepping Stones for Success* (Nashville: Thomas Nelson, 2000), 143.

3   Ibid., 115.

4   *Forbes Magazine*, online edition, January 16, 2015.

5   Dweck, *Mindset*, 29, 155.

6   Ibid., 252.

7   Jon Gordon, *The Power of a Positive Team: Proven Principles and Practices That Make Great Teams Great* (Hoboken, NJ: John Wiley & Sons, 2018), 82.

8   Ibid., 84–86.

9   Ibid., 88–89.

10   Ibid., 94–95.

11   Dweck, *Mindset*, 238–39.

12   Leo Babauta, *Zen Habits: Handbook for Life* (Leo Babauta, Editorium, 2011), 34–35.

13   Dweck, *Mindset*, 97–98.

14   Ibid., 210.

15   Ibid.,128–29, 132, 140–41.

16   Herman A. Witkin, *Psychological Differentiation: Studies of Development* (L. Erlbaum Associates; distributed by Halsted Press Division, Wiley, New York, 1974).

Made in United States
North Haven, CT
15 November 2022

26767257R10040